For the Pleasure of Seeing Her Again

For the Pleasure of Seeing Her Again

Michel Tremblay

translated by
Linda Gaboriau

Talonbooks
1998

Talonbooks
#104—3100 Production Way
Burnaby, British Columbia, Canada V5A 4R4

Typeset in Frutiger and New Baskerville and printed and bound in
Canada by Hignell Printing Ltd.

First Printing: October 1998

Talonbooks are distributed in Canada by General Distribution
Services, 325 Humber College Blvd., Toronto, Ontario, Canada
M9W 7C3; Tel.:(416) 213-1919; Fax:(416) 213-1917.
Talonbooks are distributed in the U.S.A. by General Distribution
Services Inc., 85 Rock River Drive, Suite 202, Buffalo, New York,
U.S.A. 14207-2170; Tel.:1-800-805-1083; Fax:1-800-481-6207.

Encore une fois, si vous permettez was published simultaneously in the
original French by Leméac Éditeur, Montréal, Québec.

Canadian Cataloguing in Publication Data

Tremblay, Michel, 1942-
    [Encore une fois, si nous permettez. English]
    For the pleasure of seeing her again

    A play.
    Translation of: Encore une fois, si nous permettez.
    ISBN 0-88922-389-0

    I. Title. II. Title: Encore une fois, si nous permettez. English.
PS8539.R47E5213 1998   C842'.54   C98-910721-3
PQ3919.2.T73E5213 1998

The first English-language production of *For the Pleasure of Seeing Her Again* was produced by Centaur Theatre Company, Montreal, Quebec. Its premiere presentation took place on October 1, 1998 with the following cast:

NANA ....Nicola Cavendish
NARRATOR ....Dennis O'Connor

Directed by Gordon McCall
Set and Costume Design by John C. Dinning
Lighting Design by Graham Frampton
Assistant Director: Nathalie Bonjour
Stage Managed by Johanne Pomrenski
Assistant Stage Manager: Tobi M. Hunt

The stage is empty.

*The NARRATOR enters, sits down on a chair where
he will stay until the end.*

*He can move, gesticulate, cross his arms and legs, but
he should not leave the chair until the last few
minutes of the play.*

*NANA, on the other hand, takes over the stage the
minute she arrives, she fills it, dominates it, makes it
her kingdom.*

It is her space.

NARRATOR
Tonight, no one will rage and cry: "My kingdom for
a horse!" No ghost will come to haunt the
battlements of a castle in the kingdom of Denmark
where, apparently, something is rotten. Nor will
anyone wring her hands and murmur: "Leave, I do
not despise you." Three still young women will not
retreat to a dacha, whispering the name of Moscow,
their beloved, their lost hope. No sister will await
the return of her brother to avenge the death of
their father, no son will be forced to avenge an
affront to his father, no mother will kill her three
children to take revenge on their father. And no
husband will see his doll-like wife leave him out of
contempt. No one will turn into a rhinoceros. Maids
will not plot to assassinate their mistress, after

denouncing her lover and having him jailed. No one will fret about "the rain in Spain!" No one will emerge from a garbage pail to tell an absurd story. Italian families will not leave for the seashore. No soldier will return from World War II and bang on his father's bedroom door, protesting the presence of a new wife in his mother's bed. No evanescent blonde will drown. No Spanish nobleman will seduce a thousand and three women, nor will an entire family of Spanish women writhe beneath the heel of the fierce Bernarda Alba. You won't see a brute of a man rip his sweat-drenched T-shirt, shouting: "Stella! Stella!" and his sister-in-law will not be doomed the minute she steps off the street-car named Desire. Nor will you see a stepmother pine away for her new husband's youngest son. The plague will not descend upon the city of Thebes, and the Trojan War will not take place. No king will be betrayed by his ungrateful daughters. There will be no duels, no poisonings, no wracking coughs. No one will die, or, if someone must die, it will become a comic scene. No, there will be none of the usual theatrics. What you will see tonight is a very simple woman, a woman who will simply talk.... I almost said, about her life, but the lives of others will be just as important: her husband, her sons, her relatives and neighbours. Perhaps you will recognize her. You've often run into her at the theatre, in the audience and on stage, you've met her in life, she's one of you. She was born, it's true, during a specific era in this country and lived her life in a city that resembles this city, but, I am convinced, she is everywhere. She is universal. She is Rodrigue's aunt, Electra's cousin, Ivanov's sister, Caligula's stepmother, Mistress Quickly's little niece, the mother of Ham or of Clov, or perhaps of both. And when she speaks in her own words, people who speak differently will understand her, in their own words. She has existed throughout the ages and in every culture. She always has been present and always will be. I wanted the pleasure of seeing her again. The pleasure of hearing her. So she could make me laugh and cry. One more time, if I may. (*He looks towards the wings.*) Aha, I hear her coming. Get ready, she'll talk a blue streak, because words have always been her most effective weapon. (*He smiles.*) As they say in the classics: "Hark, she cometh this way!"

Enter NANA.

She is visibly furious

NANA
Go to your room. Right this minute! How could you do such a thing? At your age! Ten years old, you should know better! No, it's not true, how can I say that, at ten, you can't be expected to know much. Maybe you've reached the age of reason, but you're inexperienced. At ten, you're just a stupid kid, and you act like a stupid kid! But still, I thought you'd be smart enough to know not to do something like this!

NARRATOR
I didn't do it on purpose.

NANA
You didn't do it on purpose?! You threw a chunk of ice under a moving car, don't try to tell me you didn't do it on purpose! That chunk of ice didn't take off by itself.

NARRATOR
Everybody was doing it!

NANA

Listen to that! How smart can you get! Everybody
was doing it! Since when do you have to act like
everybody else? If everybody decides to go lick a
frozen fence post, are you going to risk tearing off
the tip of your tongue and lisping for the rest of
your life, just to act like everybody else?

NARRATOR

If I hadn't done it—

NANA

If you hadn't done it, none of this would have
happened, and I wouldn't have been so ashamed of
you! Do you realize what I just went through? Eh?
Do you? You don't seem very upset. There I was
quietly doing my wash, pulling your father's drawers
through the wringer, listening to the radio, I think I
was even singing, and the doorbell rings. I didn't
have time to go to the door, besides I thought it was
the kid from Provost's Market who'd come to
deliver the meat, so I yelled: "C'mon in, door's not
locked!" as loud as I could, hoping he'd hear me,
and I kept pulling stuff through the wringer. But
nothing happened, so I turned around. I thought
maybe the kid from Provost's was too shy to walk
through to the kitchen…. And what do I see burst
into my dining room? A policeman! A policeman in
uniform! In my own dining room! With his cap on
his head and his heavy winter coat! Barefoot 'cause
he had the decency to take his boots off in the hall!
A policeman standing barefoot in my dining room,
how do you think I felt! Of course, you're nowhere
in sight, you're hiding in your room, so how was I
supposed to know he'd come for you! Do you know
what I thought? I thought someone had died! I
thought someone was *dead!* Your father, or one of
your brothers, or you! Do you know what went

through my mind, eh, have you any idea? Maybe it only lasted a few seconds, who knows, but I saw a corpse, covered with a plaid blanket,cut in two by a streetcar or squashed by a bus, and that corpse was one of you! All I could see was a hand sticking out from under that blanket and I had to guess whose hand it was! Do you realize how that makes a mother feel? Eh? Answer me!

NARRATOR

You're pretty melodramatic, Ma.

NANA

Don't you talk to me like that! Just wait till a bare-socked policeman brings me back cut in two under a plaid wool blanket, young man, then we'll see which one of us is more melodramatic! I could've got my arm caught in the wringer! Right up to the elbow! Up to my armpit! Like your Aunt Gertrude!

NARRATOR

Aunt Gertrude —

NANA

Forget your Aunt Gertrude and listen to me, I haven't finished! So there I am, my jaw hanging open, facing the policeman, with one of your father's drawers caught in the wringer, spinning round and round, and I felt like the kitchen floor was about to cave in and I was going to end up downstairs, lying spreadeagle on Madame Forget's kitchen table with bits of baloney sandwiches stuck to my back!

The NARRATOR laughs.

NANA

Don't laugh, it's not funny!

NARRATOR
> Don't tell me you thought about the baloney
> sandwiches, Ma, you just added that now—

NANA
> Maybe they weren't baloney sandwiches, but I felt
> them sticking to my back just the same!

NARRATOR
> Ma....

NANA
> Shut up and listen to me! I can never get a word in
> edgewise around here!

> *The NARRATOR shakes his head and tries not to
> smile.*

NANA
> I didn't dare ask him who had died, you hear me, I
> was afraid I'd collapse and die right there myself....
> Two deaths in the family, the same day, that's one
> too many! But no! Nobody died! It was just...just
> that my stupid kid had been arrested like a highway
> robber because he was fooling around with his
> stupid friends, throwing chunks of ice under the
> cars going by! Imagine how ashamed I was! Ten
> years old! Ten years old and a delinquent already!
> Do you know what went through my mind when he
> told me that? Any idea? Do you know what I saw?

> *The NARRATOR raises his eyes to heaven.*

NANA
> Don't roll your eyes like that, how many times do I
> have to tell you, I hate it when you do that! While
> he was telling me about your little...mishap, there I
> was, picturing you locked up in jail for the rest of
> your life! I could see you, my own kid, behind bars
> for the rest of your days. I saw you growing up,

12

getting married, having kids…. (*She realizes what she just said.*) I don't mean you got married and had kids in jail, I mean, I saw you spending the rest of your days, in and out of jail, and then…. Oh, now I'm all mixed up. I know you're laughing at me, and that always makes me upset! I don't feel like spending the rest of my life with a bag of oranges in one hand and a hankie in the other, every Sunday afternoon, visiting you in some jail, is that clear?

NARRATOR
It wasn't that serious, what I did, Ma, you shouldn't get all upset like that…and the policeman didn't come just because of the chunk of ice—

NANA
So why did he come, then, just to scare the wits out of me? Just to upset me?

NARRATOR
Didn't he tell you what happened?

NANA
Maybe he did, but he could've been speaking Chinese, I wouldn't have noticed, I was so upset….

NARRATOR
Listen, I'll tell you what happened.

NANA
Make it fast. You always go into too much detail.

NARRATOR
But I don't want you to punish me….

NANA
Well, I'll be the judge of that, young man, you hear me?

13

NARRATOR

Just

I should have kept my mouth shut. If you didn't
listen to him, you don't know what happened—

NANA

(*threateningly*) I promise I'll listen to every word you
have to say.

NARRATOR

yeah, And I'm gonna get it afterwards....

NANA

You were asking for it. Go on, I'm listening.

NARRATOR

Oh, God!

NANA

Don't take the Lord's name in vain! Not in front of
me! How many times do I have to tell you, it's just as
bad as swearing! You're looking for trouble, buster.

NARRATOR

Now I'm not so sure I want to tell you what
happened.

NANA

Well, now I want to know! Let's hear it!

NARRATOR

It's true that me and my friends were throwing
chunks of ice, but we weren't throwing them under
the cars. We were aiming in front of the cars, before
they arrived, to see how the drivers would react, to
see if they'd slam on the brakes or just slow down....
It was only a game, Ma...it wasn't serious.... Most of
the time, the drivers didn't even notice because the
chunks of ice were too small. Then, when it was my
turn, I chose a chunk that was a bit bigger, to make
sure the guy driving down the street would see it...

that's when Jean-Paul Jodoin held my arm. I struggled, finally pulled away from him, and the chunk of ice landed too late, it rolled under the back wheels of the car...and the guy thought he had run over a kid.

NANA

So that's the bit about the run-over kid! I knew there was something about a run-over kid! He got out of his car thinking he had run over a kid, and all he found was a chunk of ice! No wonder he called the cops! Can you imagine how he felt? Eh? Can you imagine what he went through, the poor guy, thinking he'd driven over the body of some poor little kid who was trying to cross the street! Maybe crawling across the street on all fours! He probably thought it was a baby who'd escaped from his mother and was crawling across the street on all fours! Good heavens! Poor man! You're lucky he didn't strangle you right on the spot! That's what I would have done, for sure, I would've driven over you with my car! And I'm not kidding! Well, believe you me, you're going to pay for this, I'm not going to forget this in a hurry!

NARRATOR

I didn't do it on purpose, Ma!

NANA

Stop saying that! If you weren't such a copycat, things like this wouldn't happen!

NARRATOR

It's the first time it's happened!

NANA

That's no excuse! Can't you think for yourself? Can't you tell when your friends are saying stupid things, when they're doing stupid things? Do I always have to be standing beside you telling you what to do, saying do this, that's fine, don't do that, it's dangerous?

NARRATOR

They'd played this game before and they said it was fun....

NANA

Great, here we go again! If they told you it was fun to put your neck through the wringer, I suppose you'd believe them!

NARRATOR

(*sarcastically*) Maybe it is fun to put your neck through the wringer!

NANA

Hey, don't get smart with me! Your wisecracks aren't going to work today, I'm warning you! When I think of that poor little kid squished under the tires of that big car.... And the poor mother!

NARRATOR

Ma, there wasn't any run-over kid....

NANA

A good thing, too! That's all I needed! A criminal in the family! The embarrassment! The relatives! The neighbours! I'd have to wear more than a little veil to Sunday mass, I'd have to wear a gas mask! Next time your friends talk about playing some stupid game, think of your poor mother who doesn't feel like wearing a gas mask to church on Sunday, just because she's ashamed of her ten year old son!

NARRATOR

Stop saying you're ashamed of me, I hate that!

NANA

You can't expect me to say I'm proud of you, there's a poor man who almost died of a heart attack because you made him think he left some kid flat as a pancake! No wonder he called the police! If it had been me, I would've taken care of you myself! And believe you me, it's not the chunk of ice that would be in bad shape! Arghh, there's no point in arguing with you, we always end up going round in circles, and there's no end to it. All I'm asking is, in the future, just think twice before you do something stupid like that! And if your friends make fun of you 'cause you don't do what they say, tell them you don't want to be a copycat, you don't want to waste your life doing what other people tell you to do, acting like a smart aleck, just so you can end up spending your life in Bordeaux jail!

NARRATOR

Did you really imagine me in jail?

NANA

With a skullcap on your head, and a pair of striped pyjamas! And believe me, you were dragging your tail between your legs!

The NARRATOR smiles.

NARRATOR

The other day, Jean-Paul Jodoin's mother asked me where I got my imagination….

NANA

Next time, you tell her that imagination can help a person avoid a lot of trouble! I'd rather imagine the worst and be relieved, than imagine nothing, and be surprised when trouble strikes! In the meantime, go pick up my order at Provost's, looks like the kid went on vacation!

NARRATOR

You're not going to punish me? A little while ago, you said you were going to punish me.

NANA

Were you scared when that guy jumped out of his car?

NARRATOR

~~Sure, I was.~~ *Yeah!*

NANA

And when the policeman showed up?

NARRATOR

Even ~~more~~. *worse*

NANA

Well, that's enough punishment for today. The police, that's the worst punishment!

She heads for the wings and pauses.

NANA

By the way, how did that guy figure out it was you who threw the chunk of ice under his car?

NARRATOR

The other kids told on me.

She stares at him briefly.

NANA

I guess I don't have to say any more, eh? That says a lot about your friends' solidarity!

She heads for the wings and pauses again.

NANA

If that guy takes us to court, I'll deny that you're my son, I'll say I adopted you, that your real parents were bandits and I'm not responsible for your stupid behaviour. And don't count on me to come visiting you in Reform School!

She turns to face him.

NANA

Reform School! You know what that means?

She exits.

NARRATOR

Need I say that the threat of Reform School hung over my entire childhood?

NANA reenters.

NANA

That's where they send stupid kids like you, the wiseguys, the tough guys, the hotheads, the birdbrains, the copycats, and they shave their heads and stick them in a pair of pyjamas made of burlap sacks and sentence them to hard labour! Instead of going to school, they crush stones with pickaxes, you think you'd enjoy that!? In your case, I'll tell them you prefer chunks of ice.

She exits.

NARRATOR

She'll be back. She's got something on her mind.

NANA returns.

NANA

Did I ever tell you what really happened to Aunt Gertrude?

NARRATOR

Yes, Ma, lots of times.

NANA

Listen to this. She was doing her wash, just like me
this morning, and like me, she'd reached the point
where she was pulling it through the wringer. But
her washing machine wasn't as modern as mine,
mine's electric, so she had to keep turning this big
handle with her right hand while she slipped the
wet clothes through the wringer with her left. You
follow me?

She mimes the gestures she has just described.

NARRATOR

Sure, it's clear.

NANA

Good. She says she was daydreaming, I say she's
crazy. Anyway. Apparently the phone rang and she
wanted to finish pushing your Uncle Alfred's
pyjama bottoms through the wringer before she
answered, but she got all nervous—you know how
she is—and she caught the tip of her left hand in
the wringer. So far, it's not so bad, it happens to all
of us. A little pinch, you pull your hand out, you
blow on it, and you go back to work. But not her,
she's so crazy she forgot to stop turning the handle
with her right hand! How dumb can you get! So she
keeps cranking away and the phone keeps on
ringing…and before you know it she's put her
whole arm through the wringer, and it wasn't even
automatic, right up to the armpit! Can you believe
it, she cranked her own arm through the wringer!
She's so crazy, if it was possible, I'm sure she
would've put her whole body through, and her
husband would've come home from work and
found her in the wet laundry basket, all wrung out,
flat as a pancake! They had to stitch her up, from
the tip of her indexed finger right up to her armpit!

When she came over, after that, she showed us her
operation, and I'm telling you, I almost lost
unconsciousness, it was so ugly! Imagine, she had
stitching that ran all the way up…through the fat
part of her arm, and you know how flabby the fat
part of her arm is…all she has to do is give it a little
tap and it starts shaking like a bowl of jello…. She
might be my sister-in-law, but I'm telling you, she's
no genius….

She exits.

NARRATOR
My Aunt Gertrude only pinched the tips of her
index and middle fingers, and they were bruised for
a few days—

NANA returns.

NANA
Did you believe everything I just told you?

NARRATOR
I knew there was more to come.

NANA
I'm talking to you!

NARRATOR
No, Ma, I didn't believe everything you just told me.

NANA
Good, I'm glad. You're not as gullible as I thought.
Next time your friends tell you crazy stories, and
they promise you the world if you do what they say,
just remember the story of Aunt Gertrude. Divide
everything by ten, and that'll give you an idea of
how much fun is really in store for you!

She exits.

The NARRATOR smiles.

NARRATOR
Sometimes she was the only one who understood
the point of her stories.

He takes out a copy of Patira *by Raoul de Navery,
places it on his lap.*

NANA returns.

NANA
You finished it already?

NARRATOR
It doesn't take forever to read that kind of book,
Ma—

NANA
But you had three of them to read.

NARRATOR
One day each, it's enough.

NANA
Beautiful books, aren't they?

NARRATOR
Hmmmm, yeah.

NANA
You don't seem so sure—

NARRATOR
Oh, they're beautiful. Real beautiful, but—

NANA
There are no buts about it! They're beautiful,
period. Anyway, I loved every page of them. So
don't start criticizing them in front of me, you
understand?

you go around

NARRATOR

I wasn't criticizing, Ma, I didn't say anything!

NANA

You didn't say anything yet, but I can see it coming!

NARRATOR

C'mon, Ma! I told you I thought they were beautiful! But there were some things I didn't understand—

NANA

Oh, well... If that's the problem.... What didn't you understand? Seems to me they're pretty easy to understand.

NARRATOR

The story's easy to follow, but.... How come, in all French novels, there are always some abandoned children?

NANA

What do you mean? Are there that many?

NARRATOR

If you ask me, yes. In *Guardian Angel Inn*, both kids have been abandoned, in *The Foundling*, little Rémi was abandoned, it's always happening in fairy tales.... And now, in *Patira*—

NANA

Poor little Patira, doesn't he just break your heart—

NARRATOR

Sure he does, but.... Do the French really go around abandoning their kids like that? Their books make it sound like the roads of France are full of abandoned children who are starving to death and filthy dirty—

NANA

They're only books—

NARRATOR

I know they're only books, but still, it seems to happen all the time—

NANA

These books take place in the past.... Maybe in the past, I don't know, maybe people in France abandoned their kids more than today, because they couldn't support them—

NARRATOR

Sure, but there are poor people here, too, and you don't see abandoned kids on every street corner! C'mon, people don't abandon their kids like that! I don't believe it! Didn't those people ever get arrested?

NANA

Well, as far as that goes.... Listen.... There are books where mothers abandon their babies on the church steps. Nobody can catch them that way, for sure! You can't ask a newborn baby to remember his father or his mother! Especially when the mother's an unmarried mother who dumped him there the day after he was born!

NARRATOR

I don't see how you can defend them—

NANA

I'm not defending them, I find it as awful as you do, but what can I say? I'm trying to find an explanation! You asked me a question, I'm trying to find an answer. Maybe there are lots of abandoned children in novels because it's an interesting way to start a story! We want to find out where they come from, why their parents didn't want them.... Take little Patira, when he's abandoned by those jugglers who raised him without even knowing where he came from, it makes you want to know where he comes from right away! So you go on reading the book! And...how do I know?! What kind of a question is that anyway?

NARRATOR

If you had been poor, you never would've abandoned me on the church steps!

NANA

I was poor, believe me!

NARRATOR

So, you see!

NANA

Maybe I just didn't have the guts!

NARRATOR

Ma!

NANA

C'mon, I'm just kidding! I never would've abandoned you, I wanted you too badly! But had I known—

NARRATOR

Very funny!

NANA

Anyway, things are different in France!

NARRATOR

That's what I wanted to know.

NANA

Now don't you make me say things I don't mean!

NARRATOR

You just admitted that things are different in
France!

NANA

I don't mean that the French go around
abandoning their kids, so don't you dare repeat
that, I know you, yakety-yakking everywhere, and I'll
look like a real shrew. Maybe the French only do
that in their books.

NARRATOR

Aren't books supposed to be like real life?

NANA

Now you're testing my patience!

NARRATOR

I'm not testing your patience, I'm asking you a
simple question!

NANA

What do you expect me to say? I'm no expert on
literature! I just enjoy reading books, I like
following the story and I cry when it's sad and I
laugh when it's funny. I don't stop to ask myself a
thousand questions after every sentence. I'd never
get to the end of Chapter One! I can tell if I like a
story or not, and I read it or I don't, period! What
do I care if the French abandon their kids or not, as
long as the story about Patira makes me cry! And
believe you me, I cried so much reading *Patira*, I felt
like I'd lost ten pounds by the time I finished the
book, so I was *very* happy, you hear me!

NARRATOR

You always cry when you read.

NANA

I like sad books.

NARRATOR
Well, you got your money's worth this time!

NANA
Sure did! When poor Blanche de Coed-Queen....

NARRATOR
Coëtquen, Ma.

NANA
That's what I said.

NARRATOR
You said Coed-Queen.

NANA
I got used to reading it that way, it was easier to remember. Anyway, when poor Blanche however you say it gave birth to her baby in the dungeon of the castle because her two brothers-in-law had kept her locked up there for the past six months, the heartless creeps, and when Patira arrived with his little file to saw the thick bars, and Blanche passed her baby through the cellar window, then Patira put the baby on some reeds tied together like a raft, what can I say—

NARRATOR
The whole story is kind of ridiculous—

NANA
What do you mean, ridiculous—

NARRATOR
Well, locking a poor pregnant woman up in a dungeon in the middle of winter—

NANA
Heartless creeps don't wait for warm weather, young man. They were jealous because they said she had

27

usurped, that's the word they used, that she had usurped her title of Marquise, and they wanted to get rid of her, no matter what! They were prepared to do anything, and they did!

NARRATOR

Ma! Blanche de Coëtquen spends the *whole* winter locked up in a dungeon so damp water trickles down the walls, she sleeps on a straw mat on a wooden shelf, all she eats is black bread and stagnant water, there are floods in the spring, the cold water comes up to her chin, she can't change her clothes, she gives birth to her baby lying there in the dark on her wooden shelf, with no doctor to help her, she saws the bars of her prison with a tiny little file, she scrapes her hands so bad they're bleeding, she doesn't have any mercurochrmome to put on her cuts, *and she doesn't die!*

NANA

What do you mean, she doesn't die! She certainly does die! She dies at the end of the first book, and it's so sad I thought I'd never recover!

NARRATOR

But before she dies, she's released by someone sleepwalking, she's reunited with her child *in the middle* of a fire that is devouring him and Jeanne, the crazy woman who's been taking care of him without knowing who he was, and—here we go again!—she's saved for the second time by Patira. Then she passes away peacefully, after kissing her child on the forehead and giving everyone her blessing! I mean, really! Come on!

NANA

If you didn't cry during that death, kiddo, you've got a heart of stone.

NARRATOR
Well, I guess I've got a heart of stone!

NANA
Don't say that! You're my son. No son of mine can
have a heart of stone! When she realizes, just before
she dies, that her hair had turned completely white
while she was locked up, even though she's only
eighteen years old, I thought I was going to die
myself.... Don't tell me you didn't feel anything?

NARRATOR
I thought it made no sense at all. Eighteen years old
and her hair's all white! C'mon!

NANA
Maybe it didn't make sense, but it was sad anyway.

NARRATOR
You see, you admit that it didn't make sense!

NANA
Maybe it wouldn't have made sense in real life, but
so what, it made sense in the book! And that's all
that matters! All that nonsense you read, the
adventures of Biggles, and those novels by Jules
Verne, and your Tintins, and the Scarlet
Pimpernels, do you think all that would make sense
in real life? Eh? No! But you believe it anyway!

NARRATOR
I want you to know that Jules Verne is based on
science! But not this! Hey! She's locked up in a
castle, it's not the size of Montreal, and nobody ever
hears her calling for help!?

NANA
She's at the far end of the castle, in the depths of
the moat, *in the dungeon*, it's explained very clearly,
you have to admit that.

NARRATOR

And nobody ever goes near there!

NANA

Of course not! There are pools of water and mud,
there are frogs and bugs....

NARRATOR _Ma, All she had to do was call_

C'mon! ~~She could've called~~ for help a little louder
and everybody would've heard her!

NANA

People hear her when she yells, but they think it's a
ghost! You're thirteen years old, don't you know
how to read? They think it's the ghost of Lady
Coed-Queen! There's a song about it in the book,
'n' everything! Did you skip some parts, or what?

NARRATOR

Of course not.

NANA

So you must've understood that when they hear her
wailing, they're scared to death!

NARRATOR

How dumb can you get?

NANA

Okay, I think we better stop right here, or I'm going
to lose my temper!

NARRATOR

Besides, doesn't that woman ever have to go to the
bathroom?

NANA

What do you mean, go to the bathroom?

NARRATOR

Simon, the jailer, he brings her a pitcher of water
every day, don't tell me she pees in the pitcher!
And...where does she pooh?

NANA

Are you losing your mind? They're not about to tell
us in books where people pooh!

NARRATOR

Why not? Didn't you ever wonder where she made
pooh in her dungeon?

NANA

Not for one minute! I couldn't care less!

NARRATOR

Well, I care!

NANA

That figures! You and your father, you're all pee,
pooh, snot, farts, and private parts, we know that!
You love that kind of talk, makes you split a gut
laughing! In your books by Jules Verne, do they say
where people do all that?

NARRATOR

No, but when the characters are lost in the Amazon
jungle, or in the back of beyond in the steppes of
Russia, you can guess the answer, it's no big mystery.
But her, c'mon, Ma! She spends the whole winter in
a damp dungeon! She can't be constipated for six
months! And if she's not constipated, and she does
it in a corner of her cell, it must smell to high
heaven after a few weeks, if Simon doesn't clean it
up!

NANA

I refuse to let you make fun of one of my favourite
books of all times, you hear me?

NARRATOR

I'm not making fun of it! I just would've liked to
have that information, that's all!

NANA

Well, I wouldn't! First of all, it never even occurred
to me that Blanche Coed-Queen would do such a
thing! And how do you expect the author to
describe that? "She crouched in a corner and did
her business. The jailer promptly arrived with a
shovel and removed the little pile." It's a novel, we
don't need to know that! Last year, when you read
The Count of Monte Cristo, and for two months
straight you thought you were Edmond Dantès and
wanted to take revenge on every human being
you'd met in your life, did Alexandre Dumas tell
you where his hero did that in **his** dungeon?

NARRATOR

No, I guess you're right.

NANA

And did you wonder?

NARRATOR

I guess not.

NANA

So, you see! You only wonder about that when it
suits you! You wonder about it in *Patira* because I
loved the book! You're just trying to make me mad!
Well, you won't succeed! You can be so dishonest,
sometimes!

NARRATOR

I'm not being dishonest, Ma, it's the first time I ever
asked myself the question, that's all. Besides, the
whole bit about her two brothers-in-law being
jealous, I didn't believe all that. C'mon!

32

NANA

And why not?

NARRATOR

They never accepted her because she wasn't a real
princess, and because she wasn't a real princess, she
didn't deserve to belong to their family! Do *you*
believe in that stuff?

NANA

Of course, I do! There are snobs everywhere! We've
got one right here in this neighbourhood, a couple
of blocks away, on Cartier Street! I could give you
her name! But I'm a charitable soul, so I'll keep my
mouth shut! She thinks she's a princess, puts on
airs, struts around, dresses up like a Sunday mass
day in and day out, and she forgets she came into
this world under the Jacques-Cartier Bridge just like
the rest of us!

NARRATOR

You didn't come into this world under the Jacques-
Cartier Bridge, Ma.

NANA

You're right. I came into this world in the middle of
the plains of Saskatchewan…. But I've been here so
long I feel like a real Montrealer…. And believe you
me, I don't think I'm a princess! That's one thing
nobody can accuse me of! Unlike some people I
know—

NARRATOR

Who are you talking about?

NANA

Never mind, it's not interesting.

NARRATOR

I'm interested—

NANA

Oh, I know you're interested! The minute there's a bit of gossip, you're right there…. Forget all that princess business, and concentrate on Patira's adventures!

NARRATOR

What is a real princess, anyway?

NANA

What do you mean, what is a real princess?

NARRATOR

I mean, what makes someone a real princess?

NANA

Well, she's the daughter of a king and a queen, it's a simple as that. You know that as well as I do.

NARRATOR

And what about her parents, how did they know they were a real king and a real queen?

NANA

It was the same for them, their parents were nobility.

NARRATOR

What does that mean, their parents were nobility?

NANA

You read French novels till they come out your ears, you must know what nobility is, don't make me waste my breath! It's people who have blue blood.

NARRATOR

Blue blood!

NANA

Right!

NARRATOR

(*dubiously*) When they cut themselves, it comes out blue!

NANA

No, it's a manner of speaking! It's an expression, their blood isn't really blue—but it's noble blood.

NARRATOR

I don't get it.

NANA

Listen. I'm no expert on French History, they taught us Canadian History out in Saskatchewan, but the way I understand it...when the first king of France appeared—

NARRATOR

Now, And how did he know he was the king of France?

NANA

Listen, that's what I'm trying to explain to you! If I remember correctly, he was a Louis! They were all Louis, I think, the kings of France.... He must've been Louis One, or Louis the First. Anyway, the Good Lord appeared to him—

NARRATOR

The Good Lord appeared to him!

NANA

That's what they say.

NARRATOR

(*jeering*) He doesn't usually show up in person, he sends somebody else to represent him...like the Virgin Mary, or the angels—

NANA

(*starting to lose her patience*) Right, well, this time was
special, it was for the king of France! And stop
interrupting me! Anyway, apparently the Lord told
him he'd been chosen to be the king of France, and
from that moment on, so that everybody would
recognize them, he and his descendants would have
blue blood!

NARRATOR

But you told me their blood wasn't really blue!

NANA

I'm trying to explain to you that it's just an
expression!

NARRATOR

Okay, but how can they know they have blue blood,
if it isn't really blue?

NANA

They know, because they pass it on, from father to
son! Like you, for instance, you have your father's
name, well, you'd have blue blood if your father
had had blue blood before you! Now do you
understand?

NARRATOR

So that means Blanche de Coëtquen, when her
name was still Blanche Halgan, didn't have blue
blood because her father was just a ship's captain?

NANA

That's right. And since it's frowned upon for
nobility—people with blue blood—to marry
somebody who isn't nobility, the two Tanguy de
Coed-Queen brothers can't forgive their brother for
marrying the daughter of a ship's captain, instead
of somebody more important.

NARRATOR
But when she married him, did her blood become blue?

NANA
No, that's the point! You don't get blue blood from your husband, you get it from your father!

NARRATOR
And their baby born in the dungeon, I suppose his blood was half 'n' half?! That's stupid!

NANA
It's not stupid. It comes from the Good Lord!

NARRATOR
Honestly! All I'd have to do is claim that the Good Lord appeared to tell me he'd appointed me king of Canada, and then my blood would be blue?

NANA
Don't worry, if you said that, nobody would believe you!

NARRATOR
Exactly! So why did they believe him?

NANA
Because for him, it was true!

NARRATOR
It could be true for me, too!

NANA
I'm your mother, I'd know it wasn't true. Mothers know everything.

NARRATOR
Well he must've had a mother, too! And she believed him, and you say you wouldn't believe me!

NANA

How do I know, maybe he was a hero, maybe he saved his country from thieves and bandits, from the plague and dragons! And you haven't saved a darn thing!

NARRATOR

Give me time!

NANA

Okay, stop trying to get me going.

NARRATOR

You believe everything you read in your books!

NANA

Well, believe you me, it's a lot more interesting than arguing with you!

NARRATOR

It's like your stories about Aunt Gertrude, eh, Ma, you can't believe everything.

NANA *just*

You've been asking questions since the day you were born, it's reached the point, a person doesn't know what to make up anymore!

NARRATOR

Ah ha! You just admitted it *that* sometimes you make things up!

NANA

If I lined up all the answers I've made up to answer all the questions you've asked since you were born, I might be a great novelist myself! And I'd make a fortune! And believe you me, we wouldn't stay cooped up on Cartier Street facing Mount-Royal Convent another day longer!

NARRATOR

What about the girls who go to the Mount-Royal
Convent School, Ma, they're rich, aren't they?

NANA

I guess so! You can tell by the cars that deliver them
every Sunday night!

NARRATOR

Do they have blue blood?

NANA

Of course, not! Nobody has blue blood in America!
Only in Europe!

NARRATOR

How come?

NANA

Don't ask me! Maybe because they've been around
for longer than us. If we had been around earlier,
maybe we'd have some blue bloods, too!

NARRATOR

What about your family...your grandparents were
Cree from Saskatchewan—

NANA

On my mother's side.

NARRATOR

And they'd settled here a long time before the
Europeans arrived—

NANA

I know—

NARRATOR

So how come the Good Lord never appeared to tell
them they had blue blood? How come he ~~just~~ only
appeared in Europe? I don't think that's fair! There

must've been a Cree somewhere who deserved to be declared noble like those guys on the other side.

NANA

It's true, actually, it's not fair. As far as that goes, you're right. But what do you expect, it comes from the Good Lord and the Cree didn't know the Lord. Or maybe he didn't know them.

NARRATOR

The Europeans are the ones who claim it comes from the Good Lord. Do we have to believe them? Did the Good Lord appear to tell you it was true, that he'd told all the first kings in Europe they had blue blood?

NANA

Listen, it all happened so long ago, somebody must've found proof, after all these years.

NARRATOR

Nobody's ever seen that proof.

NANA

Are you trying to tell me that the first one, there, Louis One, might've made all that up just to become the King of France, and that all the people who believed him were a bunch of dummies? That the kings of France were *usurpers*? Right up to the French Revolution?

NARRATOR

I don't know, I'm just asking—

NANA

That all the Louis, up to Louis…how many Louis were there, all together? Anyway, that they were all liars? You're such a doubting Thomas! Well, now there aren't any more kings of France. So that settles that.

NARRATOR
Yeah But there's still nobility.

NANA
Maybe—

NARRATOR
And there's still lots of blue bloods.

NANA
Not lots, but there are some left.

NARRATOR
There are lots of them in *Paris Match* magazine.

NANA
Maybe.

NARRATOR
There's even a queen in Belgium. And a brand new beautiful queen in England.

NANA
Oh yes, my pretty Princess Elizabeth who became queen so young! And her sister, Princess Margaret-Rose, too pretty for her own good! Don't you start criticizing them, you know how much I admire them! They might have blue blood, but those two girls aren't snobs, not one bit. They know how to behave, how to speak in public, and I'm telling you, they know how to wear a crown. They deserve to be noble, I can tell you that!

NARRATOR
Don't try to change the subject, Ma, I know how much you love the English royal family, you talk about them as if you'd grown up together, like they were next of kin! So, if I follow your logic, the Good Lord appeared to the first king of England, as well?

NANA
I guess so.

NARRATOR
And he told him the same thing as the other guy?

NANA
Probably, yes.

NARRATOR
In English!

NANA
If he spoke French to the other one, he must've spoken English to him! And Spanish to the King of Spain. And Italian…wait, is there a king in Italy?

NARRATOR
He sure speaks a lot of languages!

NANA
He's God! He's the one who invented them all at the Tower of Babel!

NARRATOR
Do you really believe all that?

NANA
I'm beginning to wonder, you know…I never thought about it that way. When you get right down to it, there must've been a Cree who deserved it, too.

NARRATOR
So, if we trace it back to the first king of France, nobility is something you deserve!

NANA
Right!

NARRATOR

So, Blanche de Coëtquen would've deserved to
have blue blood when she married Tanguy, even if
she wasn't born with it....

NANA

Of course!

NARRATOR

And her two brothers-in-law, Florent and Gaël, were
real bastards because they made their poor sister-in-
law suffer like that!

NANA

That's what I've been trying to tell you!

NARRATOR

Blue blood or not....

NANA

Right, and believe you me, I was happy when they
paid for their crimes! I kissed the book, I held it to
my heart—

NARRATOR

So, maybe the French Revolution was a good thing
after all—

NANA

Of course, it was a good thing! I never said it wasn't!
The poor people were dying of hunger while the
nobility, the blue bloods, were stuffing their faces!
Marie-Antoinette was gorging herself on Viennese
pastry while the country was yelling their lungs out
at the gates of Versailles, with their shovels, and
scythes, and whips and torches! We saw the whole
thing, in that film with Norma Shearer! But, wait,
how come you're talking about the French
Revolution all of a sudden? What's that got to do
with anything?

NARRATOR

Because Raoul de Navery says the opposite in *The Treasure of the Abbey*, his sequel to *Patira*.... Now you're the one who skipped some parts.... He describes the revolutionaries as bloodthirsty monsters, they're all hunchbacks, ugly as sin, one-eyed cripples, they stink like the devil, and they kill all the poor blue bloods.... They're only interested in taking their place—

NANA

Now, just a minute, don't get me going again.... That's enough talk for this afternoon, we'll settle the problem of the French Revolution some other day. If you don't mind, we'll tackle volume two tomorrow! That's the trouble, when a person starts talking with you, there's no knowing where it will end!

NARRATOR

I wonder who I get that from—

NANA

Pardon me?

NARRATOR

I didn't say a thing—

NANA

If you didn't say a thing, you said it pretty loud, 'cause I heard you!

NARRATOR

Then why did you ask me to repeat it?

NANA

To see if you had the courage! To see if you deserved blue blood! And you flunked the test, you'll never become king, so go do the errands at Steinberg's instead, there's nothing in the house for supper. Anyway, next time I read a good book, I won't tell you! I'll keep it to myself, that way, I'll be sure to go on liking it.

She turns to exit, then turns back to him.

NANA

While you're out, you can stop by Shiller's and take these buttons back. They're too big for your father's buttonholes. And ask for my money back. If he asks any questions, just say: "The woman says she doesn't want them."

NARRATOR

Ah!! I hate it when you ask me to do that!   ✗

NANA

Why?

NARRATOR

Don't you think he knows it's my mother who's sent me? He's not crazy, he recognizes me!

NANA

I hope you never admitted it to him!

NARRATOR

You always told me never to lie!

NANA

Well, that's not a lie.

NARRATOR

Ma! Is it true? No. So, it's a lie.

NANA

Am I a woman or not? "The woman says she doesn't want them"—it could be your mother or some other woman. That's what my mother used to call "a little white lie." Little insignificant lies we tell to protect ourselves.

45

NARRATOR

To protect ourselves?

NANA

Listen, if you say: "My mother says she doesn't want them," he won't listen and I'll never get my money back. But if you say: "*The woman* says she doesn't want them," he won't know if it's me or some other woman who stopped you on the street and asked you to do an errand for her, so he'll feel like he has to reimburse you!

NARRATOR

But he's not crazy, he knows you're the one who sent me!

NANA

I know, but I'm not crazy either! Since he can't be really sure, he'll give you the money back, it's less complicated for him and I win all down the line.

NARRATOR

Oh, my God!

NANA

Hey! What did I say! No swearing in this house!

NARRATOR

Saying, oh, my God, isn't swearing.

NANA

In my house it is! And as long as you're in my house, you follow my rules.

NARRATOR

Oh, my gosh!

NANA

That's no better, you just replace the "sh" with a "d" and you've got God.

NARRATOR

Oh, golly, then? Holly golly? Molly? What do you prefer?

NANA

Molly's fine. It's far enough away from Oh, my God. Now, get moving, get your gangly legs going down Mount Royal Street, and stop arguing…. Stop wagging your tongue and use your legs instead, it'll do you good. It'll do us both good! Here's the list for supper, I wrote everything out, and here's the buttons. Don't forget: "The woman says she doesn't want them…." (*She laughs.*) Good luck!

She exits laughing.

NARRATOR

Oh, goddamn!

She returns.   AGE: 16

NANA

What a night! Couldn't fall asleep for the life of me! I lay there thinking…. Looking at the clock every ten minutes, knowing how hard it would be to get up this morning…. I couldn't stop thinking about that TV drama we watched together last night. You have to admit it was beautiful, 'nuff to make you cry. ✗ The sets… the costumes. Just like Russia last century. And such a beautiful story…. Really, for me to go to bed that late on a Sunday night…. But…. It's funny…. I don't know why…it's the first time I ever thought about it…. I lay down beside your father, and for once he wasn't snoring, for once I could've fallen asleep right away without having to smack him or shake him…but I was thinking about Huguette Oligny! You know, we were talking about her before we went to bed, but I couldn't stop thinking about her—that woman talked for almost two and a half hours straight, non-stop! Here we go, let me change costumes, here I am giving a party, now I've got a scene with this one, then a scene with that one…. She laughed, she cried, she got mad, she made up, she had love scenes, she was a flirt, she was tragic, she didn't stop once! And you told me it was all done live, like at the theatre, and that while we sat there watching her, she was performing in some studio down on Dorchester Street and they were filming it…. That she changed sets by ducking behind the cameras, that she changed costumes while the others were doing a scene while she was changing costumes…. And…I don't know…. It never occurred to me before, but…I guess it's because you've started to write plays you don't want me to read…. It's alright, don't worry, I understand, at sixteen it's normal not to want to tell your mother everything…. But that's not what I was thinking about, I was thinking about Huguette Oligny…. And I wondered…. Who is Huguette Oligny? You know what I mean? We always see her on TV…. She's always disguised as somebody else…. Yesterday she was a woman from Russia, last year, in that play that rhymed, you know, what's it called, she always wore the same long nightgown and it took place in Greece…. Anyway. Sometimes she's comical, sometimes she's amusing, she always has tons of lines to say…but who is she, *really?* I mean, in real life? I know she's married, but when I see a picture of her in the TV guide, with her husband and kids, I don't find her as real as in "A Month in the Country," last night. Strange, eh? I feel like she's playing some role in the photograph. We were wondering last night how she managed to learn all that by heart, two and a half hours of talk, how does she do it, but I went farther than that, I wondered… where was she when she learned all that by heart? I realize she must've been at home, she must have a house like everybody else, but where is she when she learns all that by heart? Is she sitting on a sofa, lying in her bed, soaking in her bath? Is she cooking supper? Doing the dishes? Is it easy? Does she find it hard? Does she have somebody help her? Does she talk out loud? Does she go over it in her head? Does she enjoy learning those lines, or does it drive her crazy? Believe me, I couldn't sleep a wink! At one point, your father woke up and I had to smack him in the back 'cause he lit up a cigarette. You know how I hate it when he smokes in bed.... He fell back to sleep, and I still couldn't stop thinking about it. When actors are rehearsing their plays, where do they do it? In the studio? Do they always wear their costumes? And how do they do it? How does it work? I never thought about all that before, you understand? I watch those shows as if they came out of the blue and disappeared back into the blue! I usually turn off the television set, and none of it exists anymore. No kidding! Last night I realized that the actors only exist for me when I see them on television! When Huguette Oligny finished her two and a half hour show last night, she stopped existing for us, at least, for me, even though we went on talking about her! As if your Aunt Gertrude and Uncle Alfred stopped existing when they leave the house after our Saturday night card game. Mind you, there are times when I wish they would, they drive me crazy, but that's beside the point. But what did she do last night, Huguette Oligny, when she finished taking off her makeup and changing her clothes? Did she go out with the other actors, or were they all too tired? Does she have a car? The woman who wore all those beautiful gowns, did she step on the gas to get home faster? That woman's been coming into my home since television began,

and before that her voice was already here on the
radio dramas and the Ford Theatre on Thursday
nights, and I don't even know who she is!
Then…it's strange, eh…really late, in the middle of
the night, I lay there and wondered if she ever
asked herself the same question about me. How
crazy can you get! You know, they're there, they
come into our homes every night…. Now don't you
go thinking that I believe they can see us, you know
I'm not as dumb as those people who get all dressed
up to watch "Concert Hour" on Sunday night,
'cause they think Jean Deslauriers can see them!
Oh, no. But I said to myself, if I wonder who she is,
does she ever wonder who I am, once in a while? I
mean, not me personally, she doesn't know me, but
the people who watch her spend a month in the
country, or die in a Greek nightgown? Do the actors
ever think about us? They can't see us, but they're
staring into the cameras, they know they're coming
right into our homes…. Do they ever wonder:
"Where are they? In their living room? In the dining
room? How many are there? Do they have
company? Do they talk while we're saying our lines?
Do they get up to go to the bathroom during the
best scenes?" Or are we just like a great big empty
black hole they carry on in front of, simply to earn a
living? Is it clear, what I mean? I mean, they exist
because we can see them, even though they're not
in colour, but do we exist for them, too? Even the
ones who act on stage, they might know there are
people in the audience, but do they wonder what
those people do after? Or does the audience stop
existing for them the minute they walk out of the
theatre? And the actors who work on television and
on the radio, they have no contact with us, do they
completely forget that we exist? You must think I'm
crazy wondering about stuff like that, eh? But, you

50

see, last night I was lying there beside my husband, thinking about Huguette Oligny, what a great actress she is, how beautiful she looks in those gowns, and I said to myself, I'd like to think that sometimes, when she's lying next to her husband, she wonders about me. I'd like to be as important in her life as she is in mine. But I guess that's too much to hope for. I don't dare ask what you think about all that, I know you want to land on the other side, part of their world, I've known that for a long time…. Once you're there, if you ever manage to get there, think about it and try to find an answer for me….

She exits.

NARRATOR

She never saw the wings of a theatre or a television studio, she never attended a rehearsal, a costume fitting, a preview or an opening night. She left without knowing how it all works. It's one of the greatest regrets in my life. I would have loved to introduce her to Huguette Oligny, so the possibility that Madame Oligny might think of her from time to time, could exist.

NANA returns.

NANA

I'm telling you, there's no escaping that woman! Impossible! I don't know how she manages, I never see her coming, honestly, never! She cooks it up behind my back, then, I, dummy, fall right into it! Every time! And it's been going on for thirty years! More! *She always gets me to invite her to supper!* Can you tell me why? There's always some point where I hear myself say: "Why don't you come for supper Saturday night?" Why do I say it? Do I feel obligated because her husband is your father's brother? Do I just say it to get off the phone because she talks so loud? Search me! It's a real mystery! Maybe she has hypnotical powers in her voice and I don't realize it! It just happened again, right now, do you believe it?! She calls me supposedly just to say hello, I say to myself, "Careful, it's Thursday, Saturday's right around the corner, watch out!" And sure enough! I don't know what she was rattling on about, how she roped me in, but the next thing I know, I'm saying that good goshdarn sentence, and they're coming for Saturday night supper again! I'm stuck with your Aunt Gertrude, your Uncle Alfred and their boring daughter Lucille for another Saturday night supper! I know you like your cousin Lucille, but I'm telling you, that child sets my teeth on edge!

NARRATOR

She's not a child anymore, Ma.

NANA

How old are you now? Eighteen? Well, she's seventeen, it's true she's not a child anymore. Makes it all the worse!

NARRATOR

I know she bothers you because she's got some tics, but—

NANA

Tics?! That kid is like a Christmas tree, blinking away non-stop! During her awkward stage, every time she left here with her parents, my face would go on twitching for hours!

NARRATOR

Ma....

52

NANA
Ma, what?

NARRATOR
You promised you'd try not to exaggerate so much.

NANA
I tried, and I thought I was going to die of
boredom! Things are never interesting enough
when you describe them as is, c'mon! Just thinking
about them showing up on Saturday night makes
me want to pack my bags and take off for the planet
Mars. How's that for an exaggeration, eh?

NARRATOR
Not bad—

NANA
If I didn't exaggerate, you'd think I was boring!

NARRATOR
That's true, but—

NANA
So don't nag me. I can see it all now. Your Uncle
Alfred will take your father's place at the end of the
table, and your father's too much of a coward to say
anything, your uncle will light his damn pipe that
smells like the devil who hasn't taken a bath since
the Messiah appeared, and he'll start yakking about
Fernandel! That man can only talk about one thing:
Fernandel! Did you ever see anything like it? I ask
you! Men his age, I don't know, seems to me they
talk about Marilyn Monroe, or Lana Turner, or even
hockey, but not him, he bends our ear about
Fernandel! When he starts going on about the last
Fernandel film he's seen, I don't know if you ever
noticed, but I leave the room! I pretend I have to
do something in the kitchen or I say I have to make

a phone call, and I end up chatting with nobody at the other end of the line, but I have to do something, otherwise I'll smack him on the head! He talks like Fernandel, he imitates Fernandel's sissy gestures, and he *sings* like Fernandel! Oooff, when he starts singing with his Marseillais accent.... Look, just talking about it gives me hot flashes! If he tells us the story, if he acts out "Coeur de coq" once more, I'm gonna have such a fit, they'll hear me all the way to Ausable Chasm!

They both laugh.

NANA
I'm pretty funny today, eh?

NARRATOR
Yes, you're in fine form!

NANA
No choice, otherwise I'd explode.

NARRATOR
How would you explode? Usually, you add an image—

NANA
Wait.... (*proud of herself*) I'd explode like a pressure cooker that was left on the burner so long, you'd all have to scrape me off the ceiling!

They laugh even harder.

NANA
Ah, that feels better! Look, your Uncle Alfred might be your father's brother, but believe you me, he's not the guy who hitched the lanterns to the fireflies' backsides!

They split a gut laughing.

NANA

It's Mr. Gagnon, from Saint-Pacôme, a friend of
your grandparents on your father's side, who used
to say that. Funny, eh?

NARRATOR

Yeah, it's really great. I'm going to use it some day.

NANA

(*more seriously*) I'm sure you will. We should talk
about that.... But her! *THAT ONE!* She's been
coming to supper for thirty years now, and lately
you know what she's been saying to me, as she
leaves?

NARRATOR

I know, ~~but~~ mouths "the tea was very good" ✗

NANA

"The tea was very good." The tea! She does me the
honour of liking my tea!

NARRATOR

It's her idea of a joke, Ma—

NANA

A joke that's been going on for three years is no
joke, it's sick! Her husband with Fernandel, her
with her tea, and their daughter with her twitches,
I'm telling you they're quite the family! I guess they
don't get a few laughs every day like us!

NARRATOR

You always make roast beef when they come....

NANA

People say my roast beef is the best roast beef this
side of the Rockies!

NARRATOR

I know, but you always make it rare…. Maybe she likes it well-done, I don't know….

NANA

What's that supposed to mean? Did she ever say anything to you?

NARRATOR

Well, no—

NANA

Tell me the truth! Did your Aunt Gertrude ever complain about my roast beef?

NARRATOR

I told you, no…. I'm just saying that some people probably like it more well-done—

NANA

Well, listen to that! Would you be talking about yourself there?

NARRATOR

Well….

NANA

You've hated my roast beef for eighteen years, and you never even told me!

NARRATOR

I never said I hated your roast beef, Ma….

NANA

You've been eating roast beef that makes you sick for eighteen years, and you never had the courage to tell me.

NARRATOR

Ma, you've been boasting about your roast beef for so long, it's pretty hard to contradict you!

NANA

I don't believe it! He doesn't like my cooking!

She puts her hand to her heart.

NANA

He's going to kill me. How about my potatoes, are
they cooked enough for you? Are my peas hot
enough? Are my carrots chopped too big? Is my
gravy thick enough? Maybe there's too much tea in
it? Is there anything I cook right, or is it all like my
roast beef, awful?!

NARRATOR

Ma, I never said I didn't like your cooking…. Gosh,
it's hard to talk to you!

NANA

You go eat at your friends' houses where they eat
baloney sandwiches day in and day out, and then,
believe you me, you'll miss your mother's cooking!

NARRATOR

Ma, listen to me, please. I was just trying to say that
to my taste, that's just me, you don't cook your roast
beef long enough. That's all. No more, no less! It's
no big deal! No tragedy!

NANA

*Well, maybe, but your father likes his beef so rare it can get
up, moo, and walk away from the plate!*

NARRATOR

I know, but we don't all have to share his taste!
You've just closed the oven door, and it's time to
take it out again!

NANA

Now look who's exaggerating!

NARRATOR

But it's true. You ~~put it in,~~ what, for half an hour at 400? The outside is burnt to a crisp and inside it's still alive!

NANA

So just ask me for the end piece!

NARRATOR

Listen, when I was little, I was the youngest kid of all the families who came to dinner, so, Saturday nights, I was always the last one to be served.... You'd buy a huge roast ~~of beef,~~ you'd hardly cook it, and I'd end up with the middle, you see, the middle of the roast, the least cooked, the rawest, the cow was practically still breathing in my plate. It was red, full of blood, and it tasted like a wet facecloth! I felt like there was a cow in the bathroom and you'd just gone to slice off a piece of thigh and put it in my plate!

NANA

And you never said anything.

NARRATOR

You would've killed me.

NANA

If you said it in front of other people, maybe, but—

NARRATOR

It doesn't matter, Ma, this Saturday you'll give me the end piece and we'll forget the whole thing.... If I'm home for supper.

NANA

What do you mean, *if* you're home for supper?

NARRATOR

Well, I don't really feel like spending another evening with Fernandel's official imitator! C'mon, Ma, I've got other things to do with my life!

NANA

First of all, that's not true, just this morning you asked me what I was making for supper Saturday night…and besides, you have to keep your favourite cousin Lucille company while she blinks her lights….

NARRATOR

Ma, I'm eighteen years old, I'm not ten anymore, I'm a consenting adult and I can do what I want!

NANA

If you don't mind my saying so…you've been staying out pretty late these days…and hanging out with some pretty…strange people! You can go out when it's time for them to leave, period.

NARRATOR

And if they leave after midnight, like they usually do?

NANA

(*after some hesitation*) You'll leave along with them.

NARRATOR

And you won't say anything?

NANA

(*after another hesitation*) No.

NARRATOR

Okay!

NANA

Would you mind telling me where you go, and what
you do with those weirdos, so late at night? You
come home smelling of cigarettes, and you don't
even smoke! I'd like to know what kind of a dive
you're hanging out in!

NARRATOR

Ma!

NANA

Okay! Okay! We'll drop the subject! But you better
sit there beside your cousin Lucille and mind your
p's and q's.

NARRATOR

It's a deal!

NANA

You see what I mean? I feel like you just pulled the
wool over my eyes, just like your Aunt Gertrude!

She exits.

Then returns.

NANA

Did I ever tell you about your cousin Lucille's
recital?

NARRATOR

Thousands of times, Ma.

NANA

Listen to this. You'll get a kick out of it.

He raises his eyes to heaven.

NANA   ROLL

Don't ~~raise~~ your eyes ~~to heaven~~ like that, you're not
ten years old anymore! (*She coughs into her fist, as if*

about to begin a song.) You have to realize that your
Aunt Gertrude had been bending my ear about her
daughter's *recital* for months and months! I
absolutely had to attend, I absolutely had to see it,
she had made Lucille's costume herself, she'd
bought the material at the Shiller's in her
neighbourhood.... Mind you, I should've realized,
your Aunt Gertrude's never had good taste in
clothes, but anyway.... It went on for months! She
acted like her daughter Lucille was the first human
being who had ever taken ballet lessons in the
History of Humanity! The fact that she was taking
her ballet lessons in an elocution school, I
should've known...but anyway, I finally gave in and
promised I'd go, she must've hypnotized me, as
usual.... So I arrive, the night of the *recital.* It was in
a church basement, you can imagine the
atmosphere! I sit down on a hard church pew,
beside your aunt who smelled so strong I felt like I
was sitting in the middle of a garden of dead
roses.... It begins with some sketch about
Cinderella, with the little 8-10 year old girls.... Your
aunt leans over and tells me this is the scene
Lucille's in. I found that a bit strange 'cause your
cousin Lucille was almost fifteen at the time...
anyway, I grin and bear it.... Cinderella is really
miserable, her stepmother and her stepsisters are
really mean, she's crying her eyes out, the others
leave for the ball.... Normally, I admit, I might've
thought it was cute, I like that kinda thing, kids
playacting, but that night I must've decided to hate
it, so I was bored stiff.... I kept thinking, don't tell
me Lucille's going to play Prince Charming, her
mother told me she'd be wearing a dress! Then
comes the moment where Cinderella's fairy
godmother is supposed to appear. Cinderella is
sprawled out in the cardboard pumpkins and she's

crying her heart out, the mothers of the artists pull out their hankies because they think she's great, poor things, then the curtain in the background opens…and Lucille arrives on points, disguised like a fairy. Honestly, she was three times taller than Cinderella! And with her toeshoes, she looked like a horse trying to do ballet! Your aunt didn't dare make her a tutu 'cause she's kind of bowlegged, so she settled for these rags in blue and pink tulle, draped over a really stiff petticoat…. It was supposed to be chic, but it looked poorer than Cinderella's costume! It made her look like she was the one who should change her clothes to go to the ball! It was no magical apparition, it was a vision of horror! That's when your Uncle Alfred, the president of Fernandel's fan club, tries to get everyone to clap! But he's the only one clapping because only three of us in the hall realize that it's his daughter, Lucille, who's just appeared, and he looks like a damn fool! But he doesn't care how crazy he looks, the stubborn goat, he goes on clapping harder and harder! Your cousin Lucille starts to wobble on her long bowlegs, because her father won't stop clapping and she feels like she has to stay on her tiptoes till the applause stops! It was so embarrassing! It was no prima ballerina who'd appeared, for crying out loud, it was just a poor kid who'd taken a few months of ballet in an elocution school! If I'd had an axe with me, believe you me, your Uncle Alfred's arms would've grown shorter that night. He'd be imitating Fernandel with two stumps! He finally stopped clapping, but by then, there were five hundred heads turned toward us! Talk about being embarrassed! And then, Lucille, who's still tottering on her tired pins, takes a few steps, still on points, she lowers her magic wand, poof, the pumpkin turns into a carriage and she exits! That was it! I'd just attended your cousin Lucille's **recital**! She appears, poof, she waves her wand, and that's all, folks! Maybe she was on stage for a grand total of two minutes, maximum, and her career was over! Not everyone's cut out for a career on stage, you know! Your uncle was wiping his eyes, your aunt was holding her heart with both hands, and I was thinking: "Go ahead, die a natural death, both of you, before I feel like I have to kill you with my own two hands." At intermission, I found some excuse, a bus to take or a headache, I can't remember, and I took off like a coward! Never, you hear me, never did I tell your aunt that I liked her daughter's recital! She did everything, she tried everything, but for once she didn't succeed! Maybe it's cost me tons of roast beef, and I always get roped in when she wants to be invited to supper, *but never as long as I live will I tell her I enjoyed that evening!*

NARRATOR

And you wonder why she only says tea was good when she leaves the house!

NANA freezes briefly.

NANA

Well, I'll be…. You…. Well, I never….

She exits.

She returns.

NANA

I've changed my mind. I'm going to cook a ham Saturday night. You boil ham for ages, it should be well-done enough for you, right?

She exits.

NARRATOR
They never made up. I mean, my Aunt Gertrude
and my mother. Because my Aunt Gertrude died
suddenly of a heart attack. My mother always used
to say: "Your fat Aunt Gertrude never had time to
waste away."

NANA returns.

NANA
It could happen to me, too, you know, if you all don't
start being nicer to me. You've got nothing to say?
Usually, you react, when I say stupid things like that!

NARRATOR
I've learned to let you talk, it's funnier.

NANA
Well, look at that, the great twenty-year-old
philosopher trying to show his mother a thing or
two!

NARRATOR
I'm not trying to show you anything

NANA
(*laughing*) You see, you're not letting me talk!

He lets out a sigh of exasperation.

NANA
Apparently he just stood there puffing on his pipe
and watched her die. Your Uncle Alfred. He's a real
case! I just hope he wasn't doing one of his
Fernandel imitations while she was calling for help!
Don't laugh!

NARRATOR
How do you know he kept puffing on his pipe while
she was dying?! You weren't there.

NANA

He said so himself! He seems proud of it! Did I ever
tell you how it happened? It's awful! It was a
Saturday morning. Like every Saturday morning,
she was on her hands and knees waxing her floor,
while your Uncle Alfred stood there puffing on his
pipe, watching her. Don't ask me why she always
waited till Saturday morning to wash her floor, but
anyway. Maybe she was hoping that some day he'd
offer to help, that he'd feel sorry for her, down on
her hands and knees on the linoleum, and that
he'd say: "Stop, Gertrude, let me do that." Did I
ever tell you that woman was really naive? Anyway.
He says he was in the middle of telling her
something,.... Maybe she died just to avoid another
description of Fernandel cutting Suzy Delair's
hair.... Anyway. All of a sudden, she starts doing the
hula on all fours. That's how he put it...doing the
hula. I don't know how he came up with that, but
anyway. He thought she was fooling around, or
something, so he went on talking until she fell flat
on her face in her puddle of wax. End of story. He
watched her die without even realizing it. I always
said he was really thick. You want a glass of milk? My
stomach's hurting, again....

She exits.

NARRATOR

She never tackled important subjects directly, she
never asked a simple question when she wanted to
know something or when something was bothering
her. No, out of discretion or shyness, she'd make up
stories, she'd beat around the bush, she'd talk a
blue streak to hide her concerns, all the while
keeping an eye on the person she was talking to,
watching for their reactions, trying to read their
expressions for a kind of understanding, I guess. An

understanding she rarely found, because her ranting was often incomprehensible. People would have had to interpret her monologues, decipher her stories to understand the real meaning, but her wit submerged everything and all too often we allowed ourselves to be mesmerized by this irresistible flow of words, delighted by her punch lines, enthralled by her humour. For example, her last story, her absurd version of my Aunt Gertrude's death, had a very precise meaning which unfortunately I didn't grasp right away, I was too busy trying to understand why my mother made up a comical death for someone she had never liked, I was almost shocked by her cruelty. Until one day—it was in the spring, I remember that because it was during final exams my last year at the Graphic Arts Institute—for the first time in her life, with me at least, she opened up, all of a sudden. And for once, her monologue took the form of a confession.

NANA enters, walks over to the NARRATOR, stands behind him, puts her arms around his shoulders.

NANA
Will you take care of your father for me when I'm gone?

Silence.

NARRATOR
Uhh...yes. Why are you asking me that?

NANA
I've really spoiled him, you know, and he's not always easy to get along with.

Silence.

NARRATOR

It depends on what you mean by taking care of him. I can't do everything you do. You can't expect me to give him his spoonful of Milk of Magnesia every day before he leaves for work....

NANA

Don't joke about this, I'm serious.

NARRATOR

Well, yes, I'll try, but you know that nobody will ever ~~be able to~~ *can* replace you in his life, Ma!

She starts with pain, and tries to hide it.

The NARRATOR hesitates before asking his question.

NARRATOR

Does it really hurt?

NANA

Yes, but it will go away. It's going already. (*to change the subject*) Do you remember when I used to hold you like this when you were little?

NARRATOR

Of course, I do. But in those days, you weren't standing behind me, you were sitting down, and I was on your lap.

NANA

Hmmm, you really loved it.

NARRATOR

I still like it, you know.

She gives him a little slap on the shoulder.

NANA

You should've said so before, I've been holding back for years! When I'm gone, it'll be too late.

Heavy, embarrassed silence.

NANA
Have you thought about what will happen around
the house when I'm gone?

NARRATOR
No.

NANA
You better start thinking about it, eh?

NARRATOR
I know. But I can't. It's...unthinkable.

NANA
Nonsense. Housekeeping isn't the end of the
world. Don't worry, I'm not asking you to do the
housekeeping when I'm gone. I suppose the three
of you will chip in, you, your father and your
brother.... You'll manage, you'll see. Nobody's
irreplaceable.

NARRATOR
Yes, you are.

NANA
Oh, you're sweet. Did I ever tell you how sweet you
are?

NARRATOR
Oh, no. You were more apt to tell me how stupid I
was and yell your head off at me.

NANA
You deserved it, too, you stupid kid! But behind all
that, couldn't you tell how I felt about you?

NARRATOR
I guess so. But not always. Sometimes, when you got
carried away about nothing, you scared me. I used

68

to think it wasn't normal to make such a scene over
stupid little incidents.

NANA

It's true, I can get pretty melodramatic.

NARRATOR

She finally admits it!

NANA smiles, stands up straight.

He looks at her, he is smiling, too.

NANA

I'm really worried about you, you know.

NARRATOR

Why?

NANA

I don't know. I feel as if I've managed to get all the
men in my life settled, except you.

NARRATOR

Settled?

NANA

Maybe it's not the right word…. Anyway…. What I
mean is…your father's going to retire soon, he'll be
able to take it easy at last, he's worked so hard all his
life…. Your oldest brother is a teacher, he's got a
good job, even if we don't hear from him much.
Your other brother has the same trade as your
father, he earns a good living, he's got a wife and
kids….

NARRATOR

Ma, you're not going start up about the wife and
kids again—

NANA

No… I haven't talked about that for years, I realized a long time ago that you'll never have a wife and kids, that's not what I mean, even if it is one of the things that worries me most…. What I mean is what I just said, there's no other word…. I don't feel as if you're settled, and that's going to be one of my greatest regrets when I leave…. Not knowing what's going to happen to you. Not even being sure that something will happen to you.

NARRATOR

Ma, please, don't worry about me. Think about yourself. For once, just think about yourself.

NANA

I know, but what are you going to do with your life?

NARRATOR

I don't know, but for the time being, it doesn't matter.

NANA

How can you say it doesn't matter! It's *your life!*

NARRATOR

I'll manage, Ma!

NANA

It's not true! You've never managed! Never! You've always been a dreamer! Always off in your own dreamworld! Don't tell me you're going to spend the rest of your days dreaming about a life for yourself!

NARRATOR

Maybe I prefer that to being settled, as you say.

NANA

> Don't say that, you'll make me even more worried!
> That's nonsense! Saying stuff like that at your age!

> *He puts his arm around her waist,*
> *places his head on her stomach.*

NARRATOR

No, Let me live the life I want.   X

NANA

> You know very well you're not living the life you
> want! You can't kid me! Don't make me lose my
> temper! Everything you've been doing in that
> school for the past three years, that's what I call
> marking time! Postponing things. Playing with fire!
> You're playing with fire, that's what you're doing!
> You're doing nothing to get ahead in life, just hop-
> ing that something will happen to save you. You're
> waiting for someone or something to come along
> and save you!

NARRATOR

Well, I'm really convinced that something or someone   X
> will come along—

NANA

> Suddenly you'll realize that you're forty, fifty years
> old, and nothing will have happened, and—

NARRATOR

> I still won't be settled—

NANA

> Don't make fun of that either, I'm serious! I let you
> daydream too much! I *encouraged* you to dream too
> much, I let you read anything you wanted too
> young, I watched too many TV dramas with you,
> knowing perfectly well it was getting under your
> skin like some kind of poison—maybe you'll never

end up on the other side, on the artists' side, on the side of the ones who write, who act, who dance, who make movies, the way you'd like to! Maybe you'll never make anything of your life because I let you dream too much, and it's all going to be my fault!

NARRATOR

Don't say that! I'll always be grateful to you for letting me dream, Ma! Everything I have, I got from you! I'm melodramatic, too, Ma, I love getting carried away in the long monologues I make up, and just like you, I'm willing to make fun of everything to avoid facing reality! It's not a weakness, Ma, it's a strength, and maybe that's what will save me!

NANA

If only I could believe you—

NARRATOR

Believe me, I swear it's true. If I make something of my life, I'll owe it all to you!

NANA

And if you fail?

NARRATOR

You want me to tell you something important? Listen carefully. I'm only going to say it once: I have no intention of failing. Do you hear me?

NANA

But how do you expect me to believe you? Maybe you're just saying that to comfort me, so I don't worry.

NARRATOR

Just decide to believe me!

NANA

I can't.

NARRATOR

Ma, please try, for once.... I'm asking you to believe in me.

She stares at him for a long moment.

NANA

Okay. I'm going to believe in you. But you know I'm capable of coming back to haunt you, if what you make of your life doesn't suit me, right?

NARRATOR

Oh, yes. If you come back to twist my toes, I'll know why and I'll change direction!

She kisses him on the forehead.

NARRATOR

Can I tell you how empty the house is going to be without you? *Ma* ⨯

NANA

Oh, if you only knew how I need to hear that....

NARRATOR

The house is going to be horribly empty, Ma. We're going to miss...everything you did, everything you said, even the worst stuff. I'm going to miss everything, even the worst, Ma, I swear! ⨯

Ma

NANA

Even my stubbornness that used to make you so mad?

NARRATOR

Yes.

NANA

Even my unfairness?

NARRATOR

You're hardly ever unfair, Ma.

NANA

Thanks for talking about me in the present tense.

NARRATOR

You haven't left yet, Ma.

NANA

No, but believe me, I'm on my last legs.

She puts her hands on her stomach, and leans against him lightly.

NARRATOR

Is it starting again?

NANA

Yes.

NARRATOR

If you only knew how useless I feel.

NANA

When I was carrying you kids, it hurt there. The same place. The exact same place. That's what makes me the saddest. I feel like…I feel like I'm carrying my death. Like I'm pregnant with my own death. Like I'm preparing to give birth to my death. Do you understand? Sometimes, it's the same symptoms. I mean, when the pain starts, it hurts in the same place, a bit the same way…but not afterwards, not when the pain gets worse, when it becomes unbearable. You kids never hurt like that, even if all five of you were big babies…. I don't know how to explain it…. It's a presence, like being

74

pregnant, you can feel that something is feeding off you, something that's growing, trying to kick.... but...it's not life.... You can't...you can't imagine what's it's like knowing that you're carrying your own death inside you! And knowing, because it hurts in a specific place, exactly where in your body death will overcome you.... I look at myself the way I did when I was pregnant, twenty years after my last baby, like this, you know, with my head bent over, my hands on my belly, and I know that it's my death that's there! There, where five times—

NARRATOR

Don't talk about it, Ma, it will only make you feel bad....

NANA

Don't stop me, maybe it will do me good, bring some relief...not from the pain, but the.... I don't know...from the weight that's made my heart so heavy since I found out.

Silence.

NANA

You know what? I would've preferred to joke about all this, as usual.... You know, make up a story, act crazy or dramatic.... I tried, at first, with the story about your Aunt Gertrude's death, but.... No. I can't do it anymore. You can't...imagine...the anxiety. It's as if...you know that expression: a sinking feeling, the sense of sinking, like a ship... (*She raises her arms, as if she were going to fly away.*) ...but me, I feel as if I'm going to fly away with anxiety. The pain is horribly heavy, but I feel as if I'm going to fly away, as if I'm being lifted up, as if the fear, the fear of suffering, the fear of dying, was making me lighter. As if punishment, hell, were

above us, instead of below us! Good heavens! Maybe
I'm being blasphemous, without realizing it!

NARRATOR
No, don't worry, go on if it makes you feel better....

NANA
I don't know if it makes me feel better! I don't
know! I'm so afraid! I refuse to leave, you
understand? I refuse to leave! Not because I'm
afraid of death itself, but because your father needs
his spoonful of Milk of Magnesia every day, and if
I'm not here, he won't take it! No, that's not true.
Not true. It's death I'm afraid of. I'm afraid of
dying, there's no sense in trying to deny it. I'm
afraid of the black hole if there's nothing, afraid of
the eternal flames if there is something!

NARRATOR
You certainly won't go to hell.

NANA
Well, I certainly won't go to heaven! They don't
need a pain in the neck like me.

She almost doubles over with pain.

NANA
Help! Help me! It hurts so bad. No, no, never mind,
it's stupid of me to ask, you can't do anything for
me—

NARRATOR
I don't want you to suffer like that, Ma!

NANA
It will go away.... It will go away.... It's going away
already....

The NARRATOR gets up from his chair.

76

NARRATOR

Listen, you can't leave like this... I can't let you
suffer like this.... I've prepared a surprise for you. *Ma* ✗

NANA

A surprise!

The pain seems to subside.

NARRATOR

Yes. Come here, I'll show you.

He leads her to the edge of the stage.

NARRATOR

Turn around.

NANA turns to face the back of the stage.

NARRATOR

Everything's possible, in the theatre, Ma, and I've
prepared an exit worthy of you...

He signals.

*Magnificent music is heard—perhaps Händel—while
from the wings and the heavens a superb trompe-l'oeil
set appears, stage machinery and false perspectives,
depicting the plains of Saskatchewan with a rippling
lake in the background.*

NANA

Oh, how beautiful! Really, how beautiful! It looks
like back home, in Saskatchewan! And look, look at
the ripples on the lake, and everything!

NARRATOR

all happen

It's the stagehands, in the wings, who make ~~it move~~. ✗

*She walks toward the back of the stage, then turns
around.*

NANA

Good heavens! It's so ugly from behind! They
didn't paint both sides?

NARRATOR

It's made to be seen from the audience, Ma....

NANA

Oh, right.... There's no point.... Strange, eh, I
never would've imagined it that way....

NARRATOR

But that's not all.... Come back here.

Ma That's not all

> NANA *returns to the edge of the stage and turns*
> *around again.*

> *The NARRATOR signals again and an enormous*
> *pair of angel wings holding a wicker basket descend*
> *from on high.*

NANA

Oh, now I understand. That's for me, right? For
my...departure? My...exit?

NARRATOR

Yes.

NANA

You're sweet. It's going to be wonderful, leaving like
that! Can I go now?

NARRATOR

Of course, that's what it's here for....

> *They walk over to the basket, the NARRATOR opens*
> *the little door to let NANA enter.*

NANA

I feel like I'm going for a balloon ride!

NARRATOR

Yes, and I promise you, there's no anxiety awaiting you up there, Ma. Anxiety doesn't come from on high!

NANA

I'm not worried about that anymore, I'm too happy!

He holds her in his arms.

NARRATOR

Don't be afraid to come back, if I do things that don't suit you....

NANA

It's a promise.

The music can be heard again.

The basket begins to rise, slowly.

NARRATOR

You look good, Ma, with angel wings!

NANA

I don't know if I'm headed for heaven, but, oh, my God!, I'm having a good time!

NARRATOR

Oh, my God?

NANA

Oh, my God!

She blows kisses and waves goodbye,
before disappearing into the heavens.